LITTLE WONDERS

ANIMAL BABIES AND THEIR FAMILIES

written by
Marilyn Baillie

illustrated by
Romi Caron

Owl Books

Owl Books are published by Greey de Pencier Books Inc.,
179 John Street, Suite 500, Toronto, Ontario M5T 3G5

OWL and the Owl colophon are trademarks of Owl Communications.
Greey de Pencier Books Inc. is a licensed user of trademarks of Owl Communications.

Distributed in the United States by Firefly Books (U.S.) Inc.,
230 Fifth Avenue, Suite 1607, New York, NY 10001.

This book was published with the generous support of the Canada Council,
the Ontario Arts Council and the Government of Ontario through the Ontario Publishing Centre.

Consultant
Dr. Katherine E. Wynne-Edwards, PhD, Biology Dept., Queen's University, Kingston, Ontario

Dedication
For Charles, Matthew, Jonathan and Alexandra with love.

Author Acknowledgements
A special thank-you to Dr. Katherine Wynne-Edwards for her expertise and generous assistance.
A big thank-you to Editor-in-Chief Sheba Meland and editor Kat Mototsune for their energy and enthusiasm,
to Julia Naimska for her creative design and to Romi Caron for her engaging illustrations.

Canadian Cataloguing in Publication Data

Baillie, Marilyn
Little wonders : animal babies and their families

ISBN 1-895688-37-X (bound) ISBN 1-895688-31-0 (pbk.)

1. Animals – Infancy – Juvenile literature.
2. Parental behavior in animals – Juvenile
literature. I. Caron, Romi. II. Title.

QL763.B35 1995   j591.3'9   C94-932819-7

Design & Art Direction: Julia Naimska

Photo credits: p. 6 African Lion Safari & Game Farm Ltd.; p. 8 John Cancalosi/Valan Photos;
p. 10 Clem Haagner/Bruce Coleman Inc.; p. 12 Stephen J. Drasemen/DRK Photo; p. 14 Merlin D. Tuttle/ Bat Conservation
International; p. 16 Marty Cordano/DRK Photo; p. 18 Kevin Schafer/Mega Press Images; p. 20 David Smart/DRK Photo;
p. 22 Rudie H. Kuiter/Animals, Animals – O.S.F.; p. 24 Bill Ivy; p. 26 Margot Conte/Animals, Animals;
p. 28 John Markham/Bruce Coleman Inc.; pp. 30 – 31 as above.

Printed in Hong Kong

A   B   C   D   E   F

CONTENTS

BRINGING UP BABY

Can you remember when you were a baby? You couldn't do things for yourself, so your family looked after you, day and night. They kept you warm and safe. They fed you and helped you learn how to talk and how to walk. Many animal babies need the same kind of special care. Some of them hatch from eggs. Others are born alive, and drink their mother's milk. There are animals that look after themselves from the moment they are born, but many animal babies need families to care for them, just like you.

There are all kinds of animal families. Baby elephants and meerkats live in big family groups. Sea otter mothers and seahorse fathers look after their young by themselves. And cuckoo chicks are raised by birds that are not even cuckoos!

Animal babies come in ones, or twos, or more! Bats and orangutans have one baby at a time. Baby polar bears are often born as twins. And some animals have many babies at once. How many baby alligators can you count in this picture? (The answer is on page 32.) Now, let's meet some special animal babies and their amazing families.

BIG BABY

What's all the excitement in the elephant herd? A baby has been born! To welcome the calf, the elephants stroke him with their trunks and rumble deep in their throats. Just hours after he is born, the calf stands up to take his first wobbly step. Soon the elephants will be on the move again. With gentle trunks and feet to nudge him along, the calf will be able to keep up with the herd.

There are no full grown male elephants here, since they live on their own. The herd is a family of female elephants and their young, all related to this littlest calf. Covered in dust from their journey, they linger under a shady tree. The thirsty calf drinks his mother's milk. She will feed him for about two years, but the herd will help her guard and protect him. One young female will become a baby-sitter, for times when the baby's mother is busy eating. The baby-sitter will help teach him to use his trunk to drink and grab food. She'll play with him in the cool water of the watering hole, and even show him how to squirt showers of water over himself. Whoosh!

POUCH HOUSE

Who's that hiding in a pocket? It's a young kangaroo, or joey, peering out of the furry pouch on his mother's belly. At nine months old, he spends much of his time outside the pouch. But when he is startled or sleepy, he is safest in here. Soon the joey will leave the pouch for good. But he'll still poke his head inside to drink the milk that is just right for a kangaroo his age.

Hidden deep in the pouch is a surprise. Another baby! A newborn sister shares the mother kangaroo's cozy pocket. Naked and tiny, she has climbed from the birth opening into the pouch, just as her older brother did nine months ago. She clings tightly and suckles her mother's milk. This milk is different from the milk her brother drinks, and contains everything a newborn needs to grow. She drinks and snoozes, and doesn't mind when — flip — her brother somersaults right into the pouch beside her!

SAFE INSIDE

A long, red beak pokes out of a hole in an old tree. The red-billed hornbill has found a perfect place to nest. She has a special way to keep safe in this secret hideaway. The hornbill and her mate mix mud with their bills. They smear it over the opening in the tree. She plasters from the inside and he builds on the outside. In no time she is walled up in the nest and can lay her eggs in safety.

There is a small hole left in the wall, just big enough for a hornbill's beak. The male passes food through the hole to his mate and the chicks that hatch from the eggs. The father hornbill is kept busy feeding his whole family, and soon he needs help. The mother hornbill pecks at the dried mud covering the hole. Crack! The wall breaks open and out she flies. The baby birds plaster themselves in again, sticking up broken pieces of the wall with their beaks. Now both parents can gather food for the quickly growing nestlings. They push fruit and insects into the hole, and the chicks eat until they are big enough to break out and fly off on their own.

ROCK-A-BYE BABY

Back and forth, a mother sea otter and her baby rock in the ocean waves. She holds her pup close against the soft fur of her stomach. She nuzzles and cuddles him, gently grooming his fur to keep it clean and waterproof. The pup drinks his mother's rich, sweet milk. It's just the food he needs to keep warm and grow in the cold ocean water. The baby sea otter was born here in the ocean. Mother and baby live in the kelp beds, a thick forest of seaweed. They float just offshore, among the strands of kelp waving in the tides.

Soon this pup will be ready to learn about life in the sea. His mother will teach him how to swim and dive. She will show him how to find shellfish and sea urchins on the ocean floor. He'll learn to crack them open against a sharp rock to get at the tender meat inside. In a year, he will be ready to leave his mother and live with the others in the kelp.

But for now, his mother takes complete care of him. She makes sure he is safe, even when she has to dive for her dinner. Around and around her baby she wraps a strand of kelp. She doesn't want him to drift away while she is gone. The air bubbles in the kelp will help to keep him warm. He waits for her return, safe and warm in his ocean cradle.

UPSIDE-DOWN NURSERY

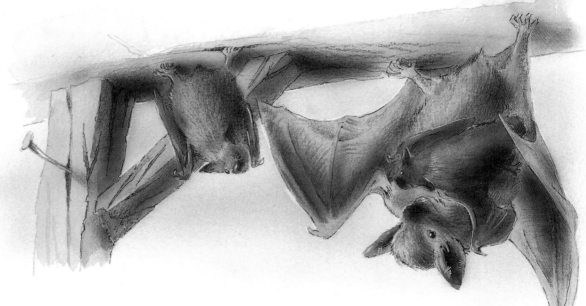

Flap, flap, whir-r-r-r! Little brown bats swoop out into the summer dusk. Shadows shaped like winged mice cross the sky. These bats are mother bats, living together in an old, empty barn. Hanging from the ceiling, each one gives birth to a single pup. The newborn bats hold tightly to their mothers for the first day or so, clutching their fur and drinking their milk. But baby bats grow quickly. After a few days, the mother bats leave the barn nursery to hunt for food. They need to eat a lot of insects to have enough milk for their pups.

Back in the barn, hundreds of pups bunch together for warmth. They cling to the wooden beams with their curved claws, dangling upside-down from the ceiling. As each mother returns, she calls to her baby and listens for an answer. She makes her way through the throng of squeaking young, following her baby's voice. Other pups try to snatch some milk, but she pushes them away. She can tell by smell which pup is her very own. She draws it close to feed it, hanging in the nursery high above the barn floor.

SWAMP BABIES

Reptile babies are born all set to survive on their own, so most reptile parents don't stay around to care for their young. But alligators are different. First, a mother alligator makes a big nest by piling plants and sand at the side of the marsh. She lays about forty white eggs in the nest and then covers them. Nearby, she waits and waits for the first little cry.

"Reak, reak!" The tiny alligators squeak as they struggle to break out of their shells. Their mother hears them, and rushes to the nest. She rips it open to help them climb out. She gently scoops some of the babies into her huge mouth and carries them to the water. Other tiny ones waddle behind her as she calls to them. The babies can already swim, and they search for snails and bugs to eat. Their mother doesn't need to teach them a thing about life in the sunny swamp. But she is there to protect them. A baby chirps a warning and they all dive for cover. The mother alligator hisses and lunges at a raccoon crouching in the tall grass. Her ferocious mouth is enough to frighten anything away!

PENGUIN DAYCARE

Icy winter winds whistle around the South Pole. All through the dark polar winter, male emperor penguins stand in blizzards of snow. For weeks they don't eat and they move very carefully. Each bird is protecting an egg propped on top of his feet. The female penguin lays her egg, and then shuffles to the sea to fish and eat. To keep the egg from freezing on the bare ice, the father penguin balances it on his flipper feet until it hatches. The egg is tucked under a fold of skin, warm and safe in his soft front feathers.

Finally, a fluffy chick breaks out of the egg. She nestles in her father's feathers, and peeks over his feet. The mother penguin returns in the spring to take care of the chick. Now the hungry father can go fishing. As the growing chick needs more and more food, both parents leave her to fish together for their baby. But the little chick is never lonely. She stays and plays in a penguin nursery with hundreds of other chicks. There are always some adult penguins around to keep the chicks warm in the cold spring air, and safe from animals that would like to eat them. But listen! The chick hears her parents' loud whistles. She pushes through the squawking crowd of chicks, whistling back. A fish feast is on its way!

TREETOP TRAVELLER

High in the leafy rain forest, an orangutan searches for her favorite fruit. She swings gracefully from branch to branch, weaving her way through the dappled treetops. Clinging to her fur, close against her side is her baby. He was born a year ago, tiny and helpless. Now he is big enough to explore a little on his own, but he still needs his mother's help to get from tree to tree.

For two years the little orangutan will cling to his mother for milk and safety. She'll teach him where to find fruit and how to get around. Little by little he will learn to survive in the forest. Even though young orangutans are very smart, it will be eight years before he is ready to live alone.

As the sun sinks behind the trees, the orangutan mother prepares a nest. High in a tree, she breaks branches and pats them down to make a floor. She makes a roof of big leaves, in case it rains during the night. A bent branch becomes a bridge, so her baby can cross over between the trees. Safe in the treetops, they curl up together for the night.

FATHER'S DAY

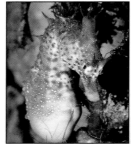 A little fish that has a head like a horse and a tail like a monkey swims slowly through the warm tropical sea. It's a seahorse carrying babies in a bulging pouch, and they're almost ready to be born. But this is not a seahorse mother. It's the male seahorse that guards the babies in his own body. Here they grow until they are ready to be born and swim free.

Whoosh! The first baby seahorse pops out of his father's pouch into the water. One, two, three, four . . . many more babies wiggle free. Some cling to each other with their curly tails. Others grasp waving blades of grass. Soon the sea is filled with hundreds of babies from the same pouch. Tiny versions of adult seahorses, they can look after themselves from the moment they are born. Up, up the newborn fish rise to gulp some air at the water's surface. The air fills their swim bladders, so that they can swim better. They search among the seaweed for small shrimp and other bits of seafood to eat, and in a year the babies will be as big as their dad.

BABY-SITTING TIME

A young male meerkat stands on guard. He sniffs the air for the scent of a fox. He scans the desert sand for the shadow of an eagle's wing. When he's sure that there is no danger nearby, a soft chirp and purr from him tells the others, "It's safe." Out of an old termite's nest tumble five playful meerkat kits. Their baby-sitter, a young female, is right at their side. She plays with them and grooms them. The kits suckle milk from her. Some day she might have her own babies. But for now she is much too busy baby-sitting.

When the rest of the meerkats return from the hunt, they bring food to share — beetles, snakes and scorpions. Soon the babies will be too big for just milk, and the hunters will let them take tidbits from their mouths. The adult meerkats all play with the babies, rolling and digging in the dry sand. Then they all snuggle together to sleep. Only the leaders of this close group can have babies. The others help out by hunting for food, keeping watch and caring for the kits. The five babies are looked after by a dozen adult meerkats — their mother, their father and the whole family.

Bear Hugs

The female polar bear digs a hole in the snow. Her den faces the winter sun to catch its faint warmth. Inside, she gives birth to twins. The two newborn cubs are tiny and completely helpless. Their eyes are closed and they are almost naked. The mother bear ate enough in the fall to last through the winter, and the milk she gives them is rich and creamy enough to keep them warm.

In early spring, the bear cubs are big enough to leave the den and explore. At two months old, they look like playful puppies. They are wide-eyed and covered in thick, fluffy, white fur. The twins tumble out into the spring sunshine. Their mother is hungry after the long winter, and wants to hunt for seals. She nudges them along in the deep snow with her nose, heading towards the open sea. Soon she will begin teaching them how to hunt seals to eat and how to swim. After two years of lessons with their mother, the twins will be ready to live in this wintry world all on their own.

Quick Switch

It's feeding time for baby birds! Crammed in the snug nest is a big cuckoo chick. His beak is wide open and he's very hungry. Mother and father birds fetch worms, caterpillars and flies to feed him. They protect and care for him, even though he is not their chick. They aren't even cuckoo birds! Like foster parents, they are raising someone else's baby that has been left in their care.

Some female cuckoos don't make nests or raise their babies. They find other birds, large and small, to hatch their eggs and care for their chicks. The cuckoo waits patiently by the nest of another bird. When the nesting mother leaves, the cuckoo swoops in, removes an egg and lays her own in its place. She flies off, knowing that her baby will be raised well.

When the other bird returns to her nest, she doesn't notice anything different about the new egg. She sees that there is the right number of eggs to sit on and hatch. The cuckoo egg hatches first, and the cuckoo is the biggest and hungriest of all the chicks in the nest. Even so, the foster parents feed and care for the cuckoo baby as if it were their own.

WHO'S WHO

ASIAN ELEPHANT

Elephants are the largest land animals, and live in forested and open areas of Africa and Asia. At birth, a baby elephant stands about as tall as a three-year-old child and weighs as much as a large man. Many wild elephants have been hunted and killed just for their ivory tusks.

SEA OTTER

All wild sea otters live in the Pacific Ocean, swimming and floating off the coasts of North America and northern Asia. They can be as big as large dogs, with cubs the size of puppies. Sea otters keep the kelp beds healthy by eating sea urchins, since too many sea urchins would eat up all the kelp.

RED KANGAROO

Kangaroos are pouched mammals, or marsupials. They live in Australia, Tasmania and New Guinea. Kangaroos come in various sizes, but the red kangaroo is the largest, almost as tall as a human. A newborn kangaroo is the size of a bumblebee when it crawls into its mother's pouch.

LITTLE BROWN BAT

Of all mammals, only bats can truly fly. They live in most tropical and temperate areas of the world. Little brown bats eat insects, but some bats eat fruit, and a few even drink blood. The little brown bat's body is smaller than your palm, and its babies at birth are the size of plum pits.

RED-BILLED HORNBILL

Red-billed hornbills nest in East and Central Africa, in dry bush and open woodland areas. Other kinds of hornbills live in Africa and in tropical Asia, and most of them plaster up their nesting holes, too. The mother hornbill stays sealed up in the nest for about a month until her eggs hatch.

AMERICAN ALLIGATOR

You'll find the American alligator living in marsh-lands in the southern part of North America. A newly hatched baby alligator is the size of a telephone receiver. In six to ten years, it will grow as long as a man is tall, and as an adult it can keep growing to become more than twice that size.

30

EMPEROR PENGUIN

Penguins are birds but they cannot fly, except underwater where they are excellent swimmers. On land, they sometimes toboggan on their bellies over the ice and snow of the Antarctic. The emperor is the biggest penguin, and its head can reach as high as the hood of a car. At birth a fluffy penguin chick is as tall as a brand new pencil.

MEERKAT

Meerkats or dwarf mongooses live in small colonies in the dry areas of eastern and southern Africa. They are the size of rabbits only slimmer, and their babies are about the size of mice. When the adults are out hunting for insects and small reptiles, the one that is assigned guard duty stays behind and watches for danger.

ORANGUTAN

Humans are cutting down the tropical forests where they live, so the orangutans that are left today are found only in Borneo and northern Sumatra. Males live alone and females travel with their young. A newborn orangutan is about the size of a kitten and is as helpless as a newborn human baby.

POLAR BEAR

Home for polar bears is the frozen Arctic. Polar bear babies are often born as twins, each about the size of a guinea pig. Cubs spend their first two winters with their mother under the snow. A hunting polar bear might cover its shiny black nose with a white paw, making itself almost invisible against the ice.

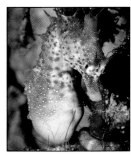

SEAHORSE

Seahorses live in the shallow, inland waters of Indo-Australia. They are also found in the Atlantic and Pacific Oceans. Newborns are only about the size of your thumbnail, but are born ready to find food and swim. Many fish fathers care for their young, but it's only the seahorse father that actually gets pregnant with the babies.

CUCKOO

Cuckoos live in many parts of the world, including Europe and North America. Nearly half lay eggs in the nests of other birds. Cuckoo chicks quickly grow big, sometimes bigger than their foster parents. Some cuckoo chicks shove out of the nest anything that touches their back, making more room and getting more food for themselves.

WHO AM I?

Here's a quiz for you to try. Each clue tells you how a baby animal is cared for by its family. Which baby animals from this book are speaking? Answers are below.

1 Through the long, snowy winter, my father keeps me warm on top of his feet until I hatch.

2 We are the only babies in a family group, and all the adults feed, protect and look after us.

3 I grow with my brothers and sisters in my father's body until we pop out and swim away.

4 My mother put me in another bird's nest, where my foster parents give me lots of food and attention.

5 I cling very tightly to my mother as we swing through the treetops.

6 Safe in our hideaway nest, we are fed by our parents through a hole in the wall.

7 All the adults in my big family are female, and they help me along as we travel.

8 My mother wraps seaweed around me so I won't drift away on the ocean.

9 My twin and I keep our mother busy teaching us how to live in the arctic.

10 I hitch a ride to the swamp in my mother's huge mouth.

11 I grow inside my mother's furry pouch until I am big enough to hop out.

12 My mother finds me hanging upside down in the nursery, and will feed only me.

ANSWERS

Bringing Up Baby, pages 4–5: There are 33 baby alligators. Count carefully — some look like rocks!

Who Am I?: 1. Emperor Penguin; 2. Meerkat; 3. Seahorse; 4. Cuckoo; 5. Orangutan; 6. Red-billed Hornbill; 7. Asian Elephant; 8. Sea Otter; 9. Polar Bear; 10. American Alligator; 11. Red Kangaroo; 12. Little Brown Bat.